Special thanks to Tony Kim for the cover art and Ron Jordan for the internal art.

NIV: All Scripture quotations taken from THE HOLY BIBLE, NEW INTERNATIONAL VERSION®, NIV® Copyright © 1973, 1978, 1984, 2011 by Biblica, Inc.™ Used by permission. All rights reserved worldwide.

ISBN-13: 978-1482530223
ISBN-10: 1482530228

Great Moments In OCD History, © Copyright, Jefferson Jordan, 2013, All rights reserved.

This book is dedicated to three equally worthy people: Tony Kim, the Korean American brother I always wanted but never had, who unknowingly, probably saved my life. And to my parents, who had to put up with so much and who unknowingly definitely saved my life.

Be sure to check out these other great books by Jefferson Jordan.

....

Okay, never mind.

Table of Contents

Preface	5
Chapter 1	9
Chapter 2	26
Chapter 3	38
Chapter 4	51
Chapter 5	62
The OCD Bathroom	68
More Great OCD Moments	71
Your Great OCD Moments	87

A Note On The Title

For those of you who donated on Kickstarter you may realize I originally said that the title was *The OCD Handbook*, though it should be *The OCD Hand (Wash) Book.* Anyway, the real name is *Great Moments In OCD History,* the problem is I didn't have the copyright at the time and didn't want some nefarious, random person to steal the name on Kickstarter and try and sell it to me. So there you have the discrepancy

Preface

I've had a few rough years here and there but 2012 was by far the worst I've ever had. I was 36, single, barely making ends meet in a job that bored me to tears, my car was falling apart and I had very little in the way of friends. I looked at where I was in life versus where I had hoped to be by this age and felt like a failure: that I would never have the life I had wanted. I fell completely apart (more about that another day) and fell into deep despair. I had, for all intents and purposes, lost hope.

In November I was probably on my last leg. I simply couldn't go on like I was and I doubt I would have lasted much longer but then something happened. My friend, Tony, challenged me to write a book in 30 days. I feverishly took it up and this book is the product of that challenge. Okay, I admit I still don't have a girl and I'm still barely making ends meet, but this book gave me something to focus on, something to pour myself into. It gave me hope.

So for all my friends and family who believed in me and my writing enough to donate to this book I want you to know you weren't just investing in this book, you were literally investing in my life, and for that I am truly grateful.

Special Thanks

I am grateful for everyone who gave on any level but some of you get special mention so here we go. Special thanks too...

Michael Jordan (for real), Scott and Shannon Overpeck, Donna Chau, Mary Grace and Ray Melick, Brian and Jennifer Griggs, Shannon "S-Lo" O'Conner, Andrew and Jenny McMahan, Kristie Richardson Satterly, Gabe Hsu (who stands before the Lord), William and Joanna McMahan, Jeremy and Dasia Ryan, Michi King, David Melick, Jared and Jessica Hernandez (especially Jessica!), Stuart "Big Stu" Whitworth, Harrison "H-Bomb" Merritt and Liz, Robyn and Joe Baran, Dustin and Tami Reece.

The Great Moments Begin

Throughout this book, I will be placing *Great Moments in OCD History*. These are moments when I had OCD meltdowns of one level or another. These are some of the odd, ironic, or even funny situations I found myself in. Hopefully you will get a laugh out of them while gaining insight into the exciting world of OCD. So without further delay, I proudly present to you...

Great Moment in OCD History 1

Generally speaking nursing homes aren't terribly OCD-friendly places. Smells, body fluids, and adult diapers are just a few of the things that can bother you, and it just so happened that I had an incident at a nursing home from an unlikely source. My grandmother was placed in a home, and every year they threw a Christmas party. There were food and drinks and a few decorations scattered about—you know, the usual attempt at trying to make a nursing home less depressing.

There was this guy serving punch out of a large punch bowl with a ladle. I hadn't received my punch yet and was in line to do so, and that was when it happened. As he lifted the ladle to pour, he missed the cup and poured most of the punch over his hand, which wouldn't have been so bad if he hadn't been holding it *over* the punch bowl! I watched in horror as all of the punch flowed down over his hands and back into the punch. There was no telling how many different life-threatening nursing home germs were on his hands. I mean, this punch had become a vat of death that would rival the Jonestown Kool-Aid.

For a few moments, fate hung in the balance as I debated whether I still wanted a drink. I had just eaten, and the punch was all they had. I decided I had to do it. When it was my turn, he handed me the festering cup of plague juice. Anxiety set in as I still had a chance to save myself. I walked away, took a deep breath, and drank the punch. I am now waiting for the blood report to come back informing me of exactly which disease I will die from.

> Now that you get the idea, you can share your own Great Moments with me at:
> www.ocdmoments.com

Chapter 1

Obsessive-compulsive disorder (OCD) is a truly weird disorder. If it were an animal, it would be the duck-billed platypus of mental disorders. If it were a work of art, it would be *The Scream,* and if it were a book, it definitely would be *Catch-22.* I have to admit, we do some pretty absurd stuff, and why not? When you think you can get Ebola from dust particles hanging in the sunlight, you are entitled to a little oddity.

If you took all the billions of people in the world and ran them through a psychological profile to determine who is most likely to develop OCD, I would have definitely been at the top of the list. It really should have come as no surprise, and looking back on my childhood, there was plenty of evidence to suggest I would one day develop it. For the record, I also developed depression, but I am not talking much about it in this book. Depression is cool and hip. It's skinny, angst-ridden guys with bad goatees who wear ironic clothing from thrift stores and hang out in coffee shops writing music. If I had to pick a word to describe OCD, I would probably call it maddening or absurd. Anything but cool.

I had a happy enough childhood, but it was also filled with fear. I was that kid—you know, the one who couldn't watch the *Twilight Zone* or listen to ghost stories because it would keep me up all night. I remember one summer we were playing outside with our neighbors from across the street.

One day a van drove slowly down the street, and one of my friends went and hid behind some bushes. When I asked him why, he said it could be a kidnapper. I spent the rest of the summer hiding from vans coming down the street.

Every kid sleeps with stuffed animals, but I slept with a lot of them, even probably past an age when I should have given them up. It wasn't just the animals, though; it was their placement. Each one had to be in a certain position and place relative to my body for me to feel safe. This was either an early symptom of OCD or else the beginning of life as a furry. Sadly it was OCD. (Have you ever wondered what you would be if you were a furry? No? Uh…me neither.)

Back when the Night Stalker was running around killing people, I was terrified he would find me. Never mind the fact that I lived in Dallas, Texas, and he was in Los Angeles. I was convinced he would find me. We had a neighbor who would mow his lawn right about the time I would go to bed. He was also Taiwanese, so I felt certain he knew some kick-butt martial arts to defend us with. I felt like he was our very own guardian angel out there watching over our window as we went to sleep. I loved it.

The point is that it should have been no real surprise when, at the end of sixth grade, I developed full-blown OCD and much like *Here Comes Honey Boo Boo*, the results were disastrous. Junior high is a crappy enough time without the added problem of your mind declaring jihad on you.

So what triggered this unfortunate event? I'm glad you asked. OCD is a funny thing. Most people with OCD can point to one particularly stressful or traumatic event that triggered it. For some it is the birth of a child; for others it's planning their wedding or the subsequent divorce. For others it may be the loss of a pet. For me it was a one-hour newscast about what would happen during a nuclear war.

At the time I went to this little Baptist school, and like all good Baptists, they were obsessed with the end of the world. The other thing you have to remember is that this was the 1980s and the Cold War was still underway between the United States and the Soviet Union. I miss the Soviet Union. Those were the glory days, back when we knew who the bad guys were and where they were. None of these sneaky terrorists hiding in half a dozen countries nonsense, and our cause was just in theory, so the threat of a good ol'-fashioned nuking was very real.

I was also that kid who loved the military. I could tell you all the different fighter jets, tanks, ships, and submarines. I had a veritable army of G.I. Joe toys and any given weekend would find me and my friends playing "army" outside. I mean, I read the *Hunt for Red October* in seventh grade when most guys were still reading the Hardy Boys. I figured I had nothing to fear from watching this newscast. Heck, I was even looking forward to it.

The newscast was on one of those *60 Minutes* type specials, and it even had a disclaimer that some of the material might be too much for some viewers. So your natural inclination would be to show it to a bunch of sixth graders, right?

It took place in Omaha, Nebraska, since the Strategic Air Command is based out of there, and it followed the lives of a family of four who lived on the base. It covered things like their lives, how much warning time they would have should a missile launch, and the likelihood of getting to a shelter in time. At one point the reporter came on and said the next fifteen seconds would simulate what would happen if a nuclear bomb hit Omaha and this was the specific point you might want to look away. I should have known to look away, but what school kid is going to be the scaredy cat in front of everyone else and close his eyes?

I don't remember the video very well. I remember the dad was working in a silo on base. Mom was working downtown, and the kids were out playing soccer in a suburb. The nuke hit, and the downtown where Mom worked was immediately obliterated as a shockwave of fire shot through the suburbs. Dad survived in the silo, but then the report showed the kids, and that is what did me in. I still vividly remember the sight of the burned and charred bodies of the children.

I immediately felt something snap in my mind, and just like a Vietnam vet, I went home a much more deeply disturbed person than I was before. I had severe fear and anxiety about what I had seen, and I knew something was wrong.

Ironically enough, some years later at an OCD support group, I met a girl a couple of years older than me. She had gone to the same school and had both OCD and Tourette syndrome. I told her about how the video triggered my OCD, and she got a shocked look on her face. She informed me that the exact same video had triggered her disorders as well. Go figure. Somebody once asked me if I was mad at my teacher for showing this video. Truthfully, no. Despite the fact it was dumb to show it, the fact is if this hadn't triggered my OCD then something else would have. It was just a matter of time.

The literal fallout of this nuclear disaster was profound. I was terrified of nuclear wars and of being burned to death. That summer one of my routine chores was to mow the lawn. I was terrified of being outside because I was afraid if a nuke went off I would be burned alive. In my mind, being inside and having my house collapse on me was a much better way to go. I would mow the lawn as fast as I could while glancing downtown. Every jet stream I saw sent a bolt of fear through me as I pictured it being an inbound missile. My mother worked near downtown like the mom in the video, and I was scared she wouldn't be able to get to a shelter in time or that she would be obliterated. The panic and anxiety were out of control.

I couldn't watch anything that involved nuclear war or people being burned. The beginning of *Terminator 2* scared the bejeezus out me. I remember one particularly painful scene in the movie *Mad Max* where a guy is trapped in a car that is deliberately set on fire. I ran from the room in terror and stayed there the rest of the night playing video games. One time a guy from a nuclear power plant came to speak to my class. He talked about the probability of a meltdown or explosion, and I was so freaked out I pretended to need to go the bathroom. I spent the entire time sitting on the toilet acting like I was having stomach issues.

There was another aspect to consider as well. Growing up in the evangelical church and attending a Baptist school, I heard a lot of preaching about the return of Christ and the end of the world. I heard numerous sermons speculating that it might involve nukes going off, so any talk of the end times terrified me. In fact, I was pretty much in fear of the entire book of Revelation. I would leave during any church service that preached about it.

One year our class was studying the book of Revelation. I was so freaked out by it that I had my psychologist write me a note to get me out of class during that time. Ironically, it was the same teacher who showed us the video a year before. I felt humiliated and embarrassed by having to get up and leave class in front of everybody. The advantage was mine, though, since I got to do a book report on *The Screwtape Letters* instead.

I don't really remember when my fear of nuclear war subsided. It took at least a few years, and even afterward I would have the occasional bout of anxiety based on something I would see. Between constantly being picked on by jocks, dealing with junior high and high school and all the junk it brings, and now having OCD and anxiety to deal with, I was as miserable as a senator caught in a scandal.

If you know a little about OCD, you might think these sound more like phobias than OCD. It wasn't all your standard obsessions, after all, and obsessions are always followed by compulsions. I did have compulsions to undo this—a prayer—but I will get into that aspect later.

At the same time as all of this was going on, my more easily recognizable OCD symptoms emerged as well: the fear of germs, hand washing, counting rituals, weird noises, zombies, and mental rituals and obsessions. Seriously, I had more issues than *Reader's Digest*. To say the least, it was way out of control, and it drove my family crazy.

To make matters worse, I really didn't want to get help. I thought I could handle it even though I obviously couldn't. To my credit, I had no problem taking medication, I even somewhat enjoyed it. However, I refused to go to support groups and therapy. My parents begged and pleaded with me, and it must have broken their hearts to see me suffer and not do anything about it. The thing about people with mental disorders is, just like addicts or philanthropists, they won't seek help until they finally realize they need it. The hard part is that you can't make them see it.

I would make a huge mess around the sink from all the soap suds I made when washing my hands and get into huge arguments when my parents tried to make me clean it. My worst habit was gargling with dish soap water and spitting it out in the kitchen sink. However it wasn't just in my mouth, I would blow it out over my upper lip and let it run down around my chin. I had to have each side clean. I would also go through half the glasses in the kitchen cabinets because I wouldn't reuse them. Oh, and I would leave them sitting out everywhere on top of that. You know you have OCD if your mom washes your mouth out with soap and you ask her to do it again.

If you have never been gleeked upon, then count your blessings. You know gleeking—where somehow somebody magically uses his tongue or mouth to squirt little drops of spit out at somebody else? Much like dating, I have never figured out exactly how it works, but you would be surprised at the distance you can get with your spittle. I used to have this "friend" who loved gleeking on me. I doubt he knew I had OCD, but he did know it drove me nuts. I would always have to find some water to wash my mouth out or find something to clean myself wherever it had landed. Totally not cool of him.

You know how there are those few people who sometimes spittle a little bit when they talk? I used to image half the people I knew were like that. It went so far that I actually thought I felt it land on me, and it was almost always on my mouth. It was horrible. I had to stand there and keep talking to these people while all the while I was freaking out in my mind. Eventually I would slip away and go wash my mouth out. If worst came to worst, I would spit on my T-shirt and wipe my mouth off with that.

We OCD types love to imagine germs getting all over us and especially around our mouths, so whenever I imagined I had gotten germs on me I would try to spit them out. Despite popular belief, even in Texas spitting isn't typical social etiquette, although I usually did it when no one was around. I was like a human llama. The problem was when I was inside and wanted to spit. Enter one of the most useful tools for people with OCD: the tissue box. I went through tons of tissues, and they would pile up everywhere. The most common place was by my bed, although copious amounts would somehow end up under and behind the bed. To this day I still haven't figured out how they ended up back there.

Travelling caused me a veritable Chernobyl of anxiety. Whenever we were on the road on vacation, I was borderline paranoid. I was so anxious about car wrecks that my OCD reached epic proportions. In particular, I can remember spitting into dozens of tissues that would pile up on the floor of the car until we made our next stop. There is no telling how much discord I caused on family vacations, and looking back I feel bad about it all.

Vacations also brought about one of the worst OCD scenarios around: the gas station bathroom. While some were nice and well maintained, there were plenty of middle-of-nowhere cesspools that gave me fits. Fortunately, for guys with OCD we have it easier. All we have to do is stand to pee and not really touch anything other than ourselves. I can't imagine how hard it must be for girls with OCD who have to sit on those gas station plague-o-potties. Whoever invented those toilet seat covers could be the patron saint of people with OCD. They are a lifesaver, and I can only wonder why it took so long for them to be invented. The other OCD lifesaver is that antibacterial hand sanitizer stuff. I always keep a bottle or three in the car.

Nowadays it is pretty normal for people to open bathroom doors with a paper towel, but let me tell you, us OCD types were *way* ahead of the curve on this one. I like to think of us as obsessive-compulsive trend setters. I would use paper towels to open doors, and if there were no towels, I would sometimes use my shirt. If I had stopped with that, it might have been okay, but of course, it gets much weirder. When no paper towels were available and my shirt was not long enough, I did what any normal human being would do. I opened doors with my foot. As far as my extensive research goes, it has proven impossible to open door knobs with your foot, and believe me, I have tried. What you can open with your feet are those swing-open doors that fast food restaurants have.

Here is how it works. Stand back, lift your leg, and hook your foot through the door handle. Then pull it open while praying nobody tries to enter while you do so. Quickly move your foot out of the handle and grab the edge of the door with your hand to finish pulling it open. Then duck out quickly and don't let the door hit you on the way out. I will say this: you haven't experienced awkward until you try to open a door with your foot right when somebody is pushing it open on the other side. It's like running into your ex while on a date. There is really nothing you can say to get out of it, and the best you can do is scurry off and hope you never see that person again.

I have also opened up those doors by reaching up and pulling on the spring-mounted hinge. This is definitely the hardest way to go, and you can generally only crack it open enough to pull the edge of the door open with your hand. Oh, and those springs are greasy and nasty. Worst-case scenario, there were a couple of times when I just stood there and waited for somebody to open the door. I would then act like I was walking out right when they walked in.

Here is a fun and embarrassing incident I once caused at work due to OCD. Most bathrooms have a trash can near the door. This works well because when you use a paper towel to open the door, you just throw the towel away quickly and dart out the door before it closes. But there are the occasional bathrooms clearly not designed by somebody with OCD, and they don't have a trash can near the door. Thus it was I found myself working at a pager (remember those?) distribution warehouse with such a bathroom. So what *do* you do with these paper towels when you are done with them? Any normal person might throw them in the trash and find a better way to open the door. Not me; naturally I threw them on the ground behind the door.

This went on for three weeks or so when one day at work the manager called all the men over for a meeting. We all thought it was something serious, like a talk about sexual harassment or our fantasy football league. Nope. They called this big, serious meeting to talk about how somebody had been throwing paper towels on the bathroom floor. I couldn't believe it.

During the talk, one of the supervisors sort of gave me the evil eye. I am pretty sure he suspected me but had no proof. The manager then said something like, "Now I don't know why anyone would do this, maybe they are afraid of human germs and don't want to touch the bathroom door." I was thinking, *Dang right I'm scared of human germs and bathroom doors, and you should be too.* They did end up placing a trash can near the door, so I won. Eventually they went out of business, so I won again.

Fortunately for me, bathroom doors were my only real door-related issue. Some people with OCD hate all doorknobs. I know other doorknobs can get dirty as well, but for some reason, they don't bother me. That's just the weird way OCD works. One thing may bother you while something similar does not. Much like life, it's all irrational fun and games.

Some people with OCD are compulsive checkers. Some have it so bad they will drive all way to work and then turn around and come home to make sure the door is locked or the coffee pot is off or the dog hasn't escaped. I once read about one woman who resorted to putting her iron in her purse and taking it with her just to make sure it wasn't left on. I read another story about a man who would unplug his coffee pot and put it in his trunk.

My checking obsessions were more or less held in check. The two biggest issues were making sure the door was locked and the iron was unplugged. I would usually check the door two or three times or run back inside to make sure the iron was off. A couple of times I would get about a block away and turn around and go back. For a little while I would say, "It's off," when unplugging the iron. Of course this soon became part of the ritual and didn't really solve anything. Eventually I got to the point where I just said, "Screw it—if the house burns down, it burns down." Maybe not the best sentiment, but it worked.

I have had some random obsessions as well. For a while there was one certain door I had to walk through sideways. I can't even remember why now, but it was something germ related. I also went through a phase where I had to make a certain noise repetitively. Another common compulsion was to blow air up over my face when I thought a germ got on it. I had a fear of going blind (more on that later), and sometimes when I saw a person with a disability, like a missing foot or something, I was afraid it would happen to me.

Once my grandparents had come over and I was playing with a neighborhood kid in our living room. He went to the bathroom, and when he came out, I asked him if he had washed his hands. My grandmother thought it was hysterical. Only a kid with OCD would ask another kid if he washed his hands.

Some people also have violent, sexual, or even violent sexual obsessions. For instance, I have read of mothers obsessing that they are going to murder their children or men who obsess that they are going to commit rape or pedophile. This may sound horrible, but remember, these people would *never* act on this. They don't even *mean* to think it. They just accidentally obsess about it, and feel like it is then going to happen.

I have had a few violent and sexual obsessions. The biggest one was at my grandparents' house in the woods of Louisiana (no, it wasn't a *Deliverance* thing). When we visited, we would often shoot guns for fun. I kept having this obsession that I was going to shoot my brother and dad. We would often clear brush with a machete, and I was afraid I would use it on them.

Another common obsession I had was a death complex. I would obsess that I was going to die or die a painful death. I would literally think, *I want to die* or *I want to die in a fire* (or something equally horrible). I would then be afraid it was going to happen and do a compulsion over it. I will get more into these compulsions later, but they generally took the form of prayers.

I didn't have a lot of sexual obsessions, but I did go through a spell during college that whenever I was around a really attractive girl, I would get anxious inside and obsess over her. My compulsion was then to mentally describe her to myself. Something like, *Oh she has gorgeous green eyes, a great smile, nice breasts, etc.* Now, I know after reading this every girl I ever knew is going to wonder if I sexually obsessed over her. The answer? You'll never know and I will never tell. Truthfully, though, it was mainly girls I didn't know who caught me by surprise, like a chick walking down the street or the cute girl at the cafe. If I knew you, I had been around you long enough that it didn't bother me. So in essence I guess I was obsessed with girls, which isn't really different than any other college guy.

Here is a list of things I have used to wash my hands:

- Soap
- Dish soap
- Shampoo
- Comet cleaner
- Dish sanitizer
- Alcohol wipes
- Spray bathroom cleaner
- Bleach (only once, though, and only a little bit)

Great Moment in OCD History 2

One time I made an appointment to see the doctor. I usually do pretty well with doctors' offices, but I do know some people with OCD hate them. I didn't think anything would go wrong until I decided I needed to go to the bathroom. I found the bathroom, and much to my dismay, a sign on it read, "Doors are locked; get keys from secretary." *That's freaking great,* I thought, as I knew what I was going to have to do. Just as people with OCD hate bathroom doorknobs, so do we also hate bathroom keys. After all, the same unwashed, germ-filled hands that turn those doorknobs also carry those keys. So I went and got the keys and went to the bathroom, but it got worse—much worse.

While in there, I *dropped* the keys on the bathroom floor! "Stupid, stupid, stupid me!" was all I could think to say. One thing people with OCD hate the most is the bathroom floor. I mean, have you *seen* the inside of a public men's room? Never before has there been such a wretched hive of scum and villainy, and I had dropped the keys on it! I decided I would use a paper towel to pick them up. I turned to grab one, and guess what? No paper towels, just a blow dryer. At that moment I seriously considered just leaving them there and telling the secretary to go get them herself, but I didn't. I sucked it up and picked up the keys.

Anxiety went off like a Chinese New Year celebration. I was so anxious, and I knew I was going to get typhoid or something. I finally washed my hands, but since there were no paper towels, I still had to touch the key. I used my shirttail to unlock the door and walk out. The ironic part of this is that it was a *doctor's* office! They of all people should know better! Then again, maybe that is part of their plan. They keep getting people sick from the bathroom key so they keep getting business, which gives me an idea. Psychologists should keep their bathrooms locked with a key. It would force their patients to do exposure therapy.

Chapter 2

In my mind, there are two perfect OCD storms, and they both involve viruses. They are HIV/AIDS and religion. I am going to talk about religion in another chapter, but believe me, it is a whole other subgenre of OCD. For now let's talk about HIV/AIDS, which I am just going to refer to as AIDS because AIDS was really my main fear.

When you look back on the 1980s, you can classify them in many categories: the Reagan years, the Cold War, beatboxing, *The Cosby Show*, Max Headroom, Jams, my childhood, and the paranoid of AIDS years. Yes, I know AIDS existed well before then, but it really came to the consciousness of public health in the '80s. After all, this was the era that brought us the AIDS quilt (1987) because nothing raises awareness like a quilt.

This was no small quilt, by the way. In case you have forgotten or weren't around then, the AIDS quilt was a giant quilt memorializing those who had died of AIDS. People would sew a three-by-six-foot section of quilting that they would then send off to the organizers. They in turn would stitch all the sent-in sections together to form one large quilt. It currently hangs on the super-large breast cancer awareness quilt rack. The individual squares would often have the victims' names and things that represented their lives embroidered into them. Sadly, the quilt currently has forty-eight thousand squares on it.

This has inspired me to create my own OCD memorial: the OCD blanket. People can sew small squares with items on them like irons, locks, bars of soap, mysterious stains, doorknobs, Anafranil pills, and anything else related to OCD. If you have a counting obsession, this will give you enough squares to keep you occupied for days, but I digress.

Back then there were a lot of unknowns about AIDS, and rumors abounded about how it could spread. For instance, some people thought you could get it from sitting on a toilet seat after somebody who had AIDS (especially if he or she had hemorrhoids). Some thought you might get AIDS by drinking from a water fountain after somebody with AIDS or if they got their sweat on you. Some silly people went so far as to say you could get AIDS by shooting up heroin through dirty needles. Wait, that one is real.

The point is that as absurd as it may sound in today's light, in the '80s there was a lot of fear and uncertainty about AIDS. Add to that the fact you might have it for months and not know it and that it is such a horrible virus and you have the perfect OCD nightmare.

This next part is going to sound very politically incorrect, and I don't mean for it to be. This is just how OCD works. In America AIDS originally spread faster through the gay community. It was (wrongfully) often seen as a "gay disease." So naturally a person with OCD who is afraid of AIDS would also be afraid of homosexuals, right? Makes sense to me. I was a legitimate homophobe. Literally, I was afraid of gays because I thought I would catch AIDS from them. Remember how I said I had an obsession about people spitting germs on me when they talked? Every time I talked to a gay guy I imagined him breathing and spitting vast amounts of AIDS all over my mouth. I could feel them crawling through my mouth and down my throat, working their way into my bloodstream.

To show you just how ingrained in my mind this fear was, in 1995 I got a job at a mall in Dallas. One of our managers and at least one other employee were gay. Oh, this was also a high-end, artsy-fartsy mall that was popular with the Dallas gay community so we had a lot of gay customers. Looking back, maybe it wasn't the wisest place for me to work, but it was a darn cool toy store.

Most of the time whenever our gay manager/coworker/customers talked to me, my mind had an anxiety attack. Many times afterward I would run to the back and wash my mouth out at the water fountain. I would sometimes half turn away, acting like I was doing something when they spoke to me, to minimize my exposure. I also had a bad habit of spitting a little bit on the sleeve or collar of my shirt and wiping my mouth off. I ruined a few shirts that way. The lowest I remember it getting was one time I was absolutely positive a gay guy's spittle got on my mouth, and I got incredibly anxious. I couldn't get away from the sales floor, so I borrowed a page out *My Big Fat Greek Wedding*, took a paper towel, sprayed a little Windex on it, and wiped my mouth off.

I always wondered if my gay manager thought I acted weird around him. He probably did. While it is better today, I doubt I could swing a gay bar even though it is probably a great place to meet chicks. Coincidentally, this is the same reason I support gay marriage—because a gay wedding has to be the best place to meet girls.

I have worked a lot of retail over the years, and I have to admit it doesn't lend itself to OCD very well. The retail store I worked at that I just mentioned was an upscale toy store (think of the movie *Big*). I had to vacuum and mop every closing shift. I hated it. The vacuuming wasn't *too* bad, but I was in a constant war with the mop bucket. I did not want to touch the filthy thing. The mop sink was near the toilet in the men's restroom. I would turn my head away from the mop sink to avoid breathing mop sink germs, only to find myself inhaling toilet germs. Sometimes I would pull my shirt up over my mouth to make a makeshift SARS mask. I really just wanted to napalm the entire bathroom.

I am not sure which was worse: the bathroom and mopping or the infant/toddlers section. First, let me just say right now if you take your kids to a toy store and want to check out a toy, don't just open it up and start playing with it. I was shocked at how many people would do that, effectively ruining the packaging and sometimes the toy. It's merchandise, people, and it needs to be paid for. Okay, I realize this whole rant probably made me look insensitive, but to be honest, I pretty much am.

You don't know what gross is until you are cleaning up infant toys and touch one that is covered in some random kid's slobber. We had lots of toys out on display, and it happened on a regular basis. Who lets their nine-month-old chew on random things in a store? I suspect it's the same person who brings an infant to a movie. Now I know it is probably impossible to keep an infant from putting stuff in her mouth, but it's still gross.

Another common occurrence was when I would straighten the plush area (that's retail for stuffed animals) and touch one that was soaked in drool. A couple of times I stumbled upon wrapped-up dirty diapers. I don't know exactly what kind of germs babies have, but I am told they are chock-full of them, like to the point of being biological weapons. Just drop a few infants behind enemy lines and we will win within a day. (Would that be considered the *infant*ry? Sorry, I couldn't resist.)

At another retail job, the manager stuck me in the men's suit department. I didn't stay long because it was all commission, but let's just say there were plenty of awkward, homophobic OCD moments while I fitted men's inseams, marked their rears, and touched the cuffs of their pants. I also got stuck selling vacuums for three months. Imagine having to pour out dirt to demonstrate a vacuum to customers. The worst was when somebody brought in a jammed vacuum and I had to clean out the beater bar by hand. The best was when a customer opened up a display vacuum and a mouse ran out. After every shift I would run to the bathroom and soak my hands in precious, life-preserving soap and water.

Then there was the coffee shop. Creative people love coffee shops. We like to hang out there and pretend to write and be creative. Since I love coffee and interacting with people, I figured it would be a good job. I also wanted a job I could easily transfer to anywhere in the country (it was a large chain out of Seattle). In some ways it was a great job, but it was *not* OCD friendly. I mean, during the interview, it is not a good sign when the manager asks you how you feel about cleaning bathrooms. I just sort of retreated to a very dark place deep inside, lied, and said, "Um, okay."

To this day I am not really sure how I did it. Okay, admittedly I did a lousy, bare minimum job. I would just spray a couple of squirts of cleaner into the toilet, turn my head to look away (and not breathe in germs), and run the scrubber around as lightly and quickly as I could. Even with gloves, it wasn't enough. Heck, a hazmat suit wouldn't have been enough. In fact, it is while working at the coffee shop that I had at least two of my best/worst great moments in OCD History. My ultimate strategy was to work my way up to shift lead, and then I just made the peons under me do it. But bathrooms were just the beginning. Next were the floor mats.

Our store was an incredibly busy store, and let me tell you, those mats get messy. Syrup, milk, water, crumbs of food, espresso beans, anthrax and who knows what else all combine under the mats to form a veritable cornucopia of germs. It is much like the Everglades but without the pythons. Of course the tops of the mats were filthy from all the shoes stepping on them, and once again, one thing people with OCD hate are shoes.

We would always wear these cheap plastic food service gloves to move the mats, but much like the French Maginot Line, it just wasn't a good enough defense. Of course there were also the mop sink, mop, dirty dishes, and trash cans.

I remember another incident that grossed me out. We used to have this really obnoxious lady who would come in and order some outrageous drink. She was really obese, had a huge mole on her face with a hair sticking out of it, and had bad teeth. She was the quintessential Broomhilda type, and nobody wanted to deal with her. She was a little crazy too, as in leaving her infant in the car for twenty minutes while she goofed off in the coffee shop kind of crazy.

The first time I waited on her, I rang her up and told her the total. Then she pulled down her T-shirt collar, reached down into her bra, and pulled out a wad of nasty dollar bills. Look, I would have had no problem with this if it had been some hot twenty-something girl—in fact, I might have put a few dollars back in her bra to help her out—but it wasn't. I froze for a second, unsure of what to do. I *really* didn't want to touch it. I almost told her to take the drink because it was on the house, but then I figured she would just keep doing that for free drinks. I finally sucked it up, took the money, gave her the change, and immediately went to the back to detox.

In my defense, when I came back, my co-worker who had seen the whole thing told me she wouldn't have touched the money either. Then again, maybe my co-worker had OCD. She was also a stoner who wanted to be a blood splatter analyst like *Dexter,* so who really knows. Let's just say, though, money is one of those other things people with OCD hate, so it is just as well that I don't have any.

It wasn't all bad. It served as a sort of exposure therapy for me. If you are unfamiliar with exposure therapy, it is a common treatment for OCD and other phobias. You basically expose yourself to whatever you are afraid of. If you are afraid of germs, you touch something dirty and then go as long as you can without washing your hands. Eventually your mind disassociates your fear as the anxiety gets less and less. If you are afraid of dirty doorknobs then touch a doorknob as long as you can without washing your hands. If you are afraid of girls, then expose yourself to girls. This is really the only time exposing yourself to girls is acceptable.

The point is all the exposure to the nasty stuff at the coffee shop was that it forced me to face a lot of obsessions. Eventually the mats didn't really bother me anymore. Don't get me wrong, I still wore gloves (everyone did), and I washed my hands afterward (everyone did), but the anxiety went away. The trash anxiety also got better. I never did overcome my fear of cleaning the bathroom and probably never will.

It is funny because I volunteer with a group called Laundry Love that does laundry for the homeless and families in need. Overall it has been one of the most rewarding things I have ever done, but I am a little embarrassed that being around the homeless sometimes bothers my OCD. Don't get me wrong, I love them and consider them my friends, but sometimes they can be dirty or seem a little sick. (Not all—some of them don't even look homeless.)

We shake hands and talk and try to make them feel like human beings again. But occasionally after shaking hands, I have an intense desire to wash them. I remember once one of the homeless guys I was talking to coughed on me and said he was sorry and that he was just getting over pneumonia. That made for a long night. In fact, I think that time I did go to the car, grab a bottle of hand sanitizer, and wash my mouth off because I was certain that besides pneumonia he probably had at least two out of three strands of hepatitis. Besides, I had pneumonia once as a kid, and believe me, you do *not* want it. The ironic thing about working with the homeless is that sometimes I feel like I am about one missed prescription from joining them. At least if I did I would know where to get my laundry done.

Here is a fun list of things people with OCD hate:

- shoes, especially the bottom
- bathroom floors
- mysterious sticky substances
- known sticky substances
- crumbs on tables
- gum under tables
- anything in the bathroom
- unknown stains
- door handles
- irons/coffee pots (anything that can be left plugged in)
- bumps in the road (some people imagine bumps being a person or animal they hit)
- wet surfaces
- spittle
- random pieces of hair
- chain letters
- cuts/scabs on people
- Band-Aids
- people sneezing or coughing
- bathroom door keys at gas stations
- smudges on windows
- doctors' offices
- bowling alleys (shoes, balls, generally greasiness)
- dollars and loose change
- airport security (those bins are gross)
- David Hasselhoff

Great Moment in OCD History 3

This great moment happened when I worked at the coffee shop. One day my manager asked me if I could change the toilet paper in the women's restroom. Now I don't like changing the toilet paper. I don't like touching the dispenser that is right next to the toilet and undoubtedly covered in fecal germs. That being said, I had learned to do it without too much anxiety. However, this time something went terribly, terribly wrong.

As I was pulling out the plastic tube you load the toilet paper onto, I fumbled and dropped it. Immediately everything went into slow motion like a scene in a war movie. "Noooooooooooo!" I yelled as my hand reached out desperately to grab it, but I was too slow. I watched in horror as it plunged into the toilet, diving to the bottom before it floated to the top.

What could I possibly do? I couldn't reach into any toilet, let alone a public one. It mocked me as I stared at it for a minute, contemplating the possibility of flushing it. I finally decided it would probably clog the toilet (a bigger mess I would probably have to clean), plus I would have to explain to my manager exactly what happened to the plastic tube. I also had the thought I could use a pair of the pastry tongs to pull it out, but that would forever contaminate the tongs. I only had one real option. I had to reach in and pull it out.

I went and put on latex cleaning gloves (which are also germ filled) and pulled it out. I ran water over it to clean it as best as possible, put the toilet paper on it, and placed it back in the dispenser. I then washed my hands like a surgeon washing for the very first time and sprayed dish sanitizer on them. I should be proud of this one, though, because one of my co-workers offered to pull it out for me, but I knew it was something I had to do. Still, if I die from yellow fever you will know why. Don't send flowers; just make a donation to Laundry Love Santa Ana on my behalf.

Chapter 3

Earlier I stated that the two perfect storms for OCD were AIDS and religion. I think I covered AIDS ad nauseam; now let's hit up religion. First of all, I am a devout Christian. Not only that, but I grew up in the heart of the Bible Belt in Dallas, Texas. My dad was a chaplain, and the very reason we moved to Dallas was so he could go to seminary. We went to an evangelical church every Sunday, and most of my schooling took place at a Baptist school. The point is I have been surrounded by religion all my life, and when you add in a dash of OCD, it gets really weird really fast.

Religion offers the perfect out for people with OCD. In fact, it has its own subcategory of OCD called scrupulosity. The thing you must remember about OCD is that there are two parts to it: obsessions followed by compulsions. Fear of germs is the obsession. Then the anxiety sets in, so to "undo" it, you do the compulsion, in this case hand washing. The problem is it usually doesn't feel right the first time, so you do it over and over. Religion gives people with OCD the perfect compulsions. Not only that, but it gives us our very own special set of obsessions. They are usually spiritual and involve blasphemous thoughts, such as fears of going to hell, feeling unforgiven, or that you have done something sinful.

Here are some examples from my life. I used to obsessively think that I *wanted* to go to hell. I would literally think in my mind the phrase, "I want to go to hell." Do I want to go to hell? Of course not. But the fact that I thought this would fill me with fear and anxiety, and I thought God was going to send me to hell for that. The compulsion to undo all of this for me took the form of prayer. I would pray for my salvation again and again and again. Sometimes it would only be a couple of times, but sometimes it would be several. Not only that, but it would have to be an exact set of words said in an exact way or it wouldn't work. Also during that time I couldn't think of anything else (which usually meant not thinking something else blasphemous during the prayer). If I did, which I usually did, then I had to start *all* over again, as well as say a prayer about the new thought. So you can see what a brutal cycle OCD can be. This is why it is a catch-22; the very thing you are compelled to do only makes it worse.

Here are some of the other things I would think as well: *I worship Satan, I am going to hell and will be left behind (when Christ returns), I curse the Holy Spirit/God, I am going to take the mark of the beast* or *I am not a Christian.* Okay, this one is embarrassing: *I want to have sex with Jesus.* Yeah, yeah, go ahead and laugh. I will have you know blasphemous sexual thoughts are not uncommon. I have read of both men and women having sexual obsessions about Jesus. I have also read about Catholics who have sexual obsessions over the Virgin Mary.

I am sure there were other blasphemous thoughts I had, but I can't remember them. The point is, just try to imagine how horrible this is for a person of faith. Even if you are an atheist, you can probably imagine just how horrible this would be for somebody who truly believes in a particular religion. Speaking of which, I haven't read of any atheist scrupulosity. Do they obsess over accidentally thinking, *There is a God, I believe in Jesus* or *I want to be a Christian*? (Actually, they do have obsessions, but it is anxiety that they are a "good" person or following the right moral code or ethics.)

If you think about it, most religions have traditions and rituals they perform. These are the perfect compulsions for someone with OCD. Rigid prayers became my compulsion (even now I struggle with this one). I have heard of Catholics who would repeat dozens of Hail Mary's or who would go to confession over and over. Imagine the poor priest! "Well, here comes Chuck for the eighth time today to confess his thoughts about urinating on a crucifix." While I haven't read much about it, I am sure there must be Jews who think blasphemous things about God and the Torah and Muslims who think blasphemous things about Muhammad and the Quran. I have no clue what a Buddhist would obsess over, and I think Scientology must be a separate mental disorder all on its own, which is ironic since they deny the existence of mental disorders.

The thing is, OCD and religion is such a mental cluster frak (yes, I watch *BSG*), and there is no easy way out. Imagine truly thinking you are going to hell and not wanting to. I have found that doing therapy for this is the absolute most difficult kind I have ever done. Essentially you treat the mental obsessions the same way you treat the physical ones. You expose yourself to them and don't do the compulsions. Just like you would touch a dirty doorknob and not wash your hands, so with mental obsessions you would think (or sometimes say out loud) your blasphemous thoughts and not do your compulsion. I would have to sit there and think, *I worship Satan*, and not pray for forgiveness. I kid you not, it is the absolute most difficult thing to overcome. One of my therapists actually got me touch the bathroom floor once (how I don't know) and it is still easier than this. It's one thing to touch a doorknob and think you are getting AIDS. At least you die and go to heaven. It is entirely another matter to deliberately do something you think will damn you to eternal hell. Even now I still struggle with those thoughts.

Most people don't realize there is a mental side to OCD. Everybody thinks it is all hand washing and lock checking. To me the mental side is the far greater hell to live in than the physical side. It's a constant thorn in the flesh, so to speak.

Religious obsessions were not my only naughty thoughts. I had plenty of others, and my compulsion was the same. I had to "pray" about it. The biggest one I remember was a fear of going blind or being burned alive (going back to the nuclear war fear from the first chapter). I would think, *I am going to go blind,* or even *I want to go blind*, and the same thing for being burned, dying in the nuclear war or other bad things. My answer to this was to apologize to God in a rigid set of words that went something like this:

I confess my sin of thinking I want to go blind (or burn or accidentally shoot my family or whatever I obsessed over). I don't want to go blind. You know I don't want to go blind. I didn't mean it, and please forgive me and spare me from going blind. In Jesus name I pray, your will be done, amen.

I would repeat that as many times as need be. If I thought a blasphemous obsession, then I would say a similar prayer but for forgiveness and salvation. The thing is I deep down inside I don't believe you can lose your salvation, it is just OCD makes you *feel* like you can.

I used to have a long prayer for protection I would say every day. It involved asking for protection for me, my family and friends, and yes, even my cat. I asked for protection from a long list of things that ranged from being burned to catching diseases to being hit by a car and even inclement weather. I had a whole obsessive shopping cart filled with possibilities. I would say it several times until I got it "right." The whole thing was a little crazy, but that is just the beginning because, of course, it gets worse.

I started saying these prayers out loud, as in muttering to myself really fast and saying them as fast as I could so I didn't think anything else while doing it. The bad thing is, I would often do it in public. I tried not to when people were around, but I know people saw. I certainly did it around my family. My dad would always try to get me to quit by interrupting me. Of course this would just make me want to do it again. It became a weird game of me trying finish before he caught me.

I would also walk down the hall in college or hide in the back stockroom at work and do it. Once a co-worker caught me and asked what was up. I told him I was praying. Yeah, that's another really awkward conversation. It was bad. People probably thought I was a psycho or schizophrenic or something. My dad talked to me a few times about it, but I wouldn't listen. I am sure my parents hated seeing me go through it, and I am sure it hurt me socially, especially if a girl I was interested in saw me.

Generally speaking the Bible is a pretty OCD-friendly book (except my old fear of Revelation), but that being said, there is one verse that strikes fear into the very core of people with religious obsessions:

And so I tell you, every kind of sin and slander can be forgiven, but blasphemy against the Spirit will not be forgiven. Anyone who speaks a word against the Son of Man will be forgiven, but anyone who speaks against the Holy Spirit will not be forgiven, either in this age or in the age to come (NIV).

First, the fact that there is an unforgivable sin is pretty terrifying on its own. Second, there is no clear definition of what all this sin exactly entails, so it is perfect for people with OCD. We fear we have blasphemed the Holy Spirit like nobody's business and now we can't be forgiven.

Now for those of you with OCD reading this who didn't know about this verse, I probably just gave you an anxiety attack, and for that I apologize. The blasphemy in those verses was that people were accusing Christ of performing miracles by the power of Satan. However, I have heard another expanded interpretation that I will share with you.

One of the roles the Holy Spirit plays is to convict people of their sins so they will turn to Jesus. Jesus was out performing miracles one day when some religious leaders accused him of performing miracles by Satan's power instead of God's. By attributing Christ's work to Satan, they were essentially denying the work of the Holy Spirit, which is convicting people about Christ. In other words, their sin was denying that conviction, or unbelief in Jesus, which is unforgivable because you must believe to be saved. The mere fact a person believes in Christ means he or she can't commit unbelief. Not to mention people who do commit these kinds of things don't generally worry about it. The fact that you do worry speaks volumes to your faith. So there you go—your theology for the day.

I have to admit, I think it must have been really hard being Jewish with OCD back in the day. The Torah has so many rituals and rules that it would drive a person with OCD nuts. For instance, did I get too close to that gentile? Did I just make myself unclean? There are rules about if mold is found in your home, you have to ceremonially cleanse it and in seven days have a priest declare it clean. I can see poor guy going back to the priest over and over, worried he is unclean. If I didn't know better, I would think some of the Law was written by a person with OCD.

One of my pet peeves is that when I would come to people and tell them the blasphemous thoughts in relation to OCD, they would say something like, "Oh, you just need more faith," or even, "God understands and knows you didn't mean it." The problem isn't one of faith, and while God knows I didn't mean it, that isn't how it works.

Nowadays most Christians recognize this fact, but that wasn't always the case. Back in the day when somebody struggled with OCD or depression, Christians would often try to treat it spiritually. They would say things like, "Pray for more faith," or "Just trust God," and "You need the joy of the Lord" and other nice catchphrases. I would then resist the urge to punch them in the neck. These people were spiritually trying to treat a medical condition. Can you treat diabetes or cancer spiritually?

Even recently I saw a website for a Christian counseling service that when asked to address OCD on a forum, listed this little gem: "The Bible says worry is a sin. We are not to worry but trust God and be free in him. His Holy Spirit will help you be free."

This is the absolute grossest misunderstanding of OCD I have ever heard and it hacks me off. To suggest that the anxiety caused by OCD is the same as the sin of worrying is absurd and shows how little some people understand OCD. Trusting God does not make it better. Scientifically proven methods make it better. God can be a source of encouragement and strength but he does not cure it. I am convinced God does not count OCD worries as the sinful kind because it's a medical condition and he understands that. For you religious people who have been fed this garbage stop believing the lies and be free. Oh, and go do some therapy instead.

The problem is mental disorders *can* affect you spiritually, so you can easily fall into the temptation of trying to treat it spiritually. It is frustrating to people like me because when we keep getting sucked into treating it spiritually and it doesn't get better, we wonder what is wrong with our faith. Is it our fault, or is God not helping us? Does God even care? Heck, even now at times I still get sucked back into thinking that way. You have to constantly remind yourself who you are, what you are, and what you have.

I would like to go on record here and say that this is not a condemnation of Christian counseling or therapy. I have personally been treated by, and friends with, many solid Christian counselors who really knew their stuff. It is just like any other trade, some are really good and some are really bad. The problem with counselors though, is that the bad ones can really jack you up, so use wisdom and really listen to what they are saying and make sure it checks out with what you know.

I used to get really angry at God about my OCD. I would think all sorts of horrible thoughts about him, and I took everything out on him. I blamed him for my OCD. I said it was his fault or wondered why he allowed this to happen to me. Sometimes I still get angry at him. I guess that is just the way it is.

One time a preacher who was very influential in my life preached a sermon on pain and bad things happening to good people. He spoke of the usual things, like God's sovereignty, how he is control and all things happen for a reason, and then he referenced the book of Job, arguably the scariest book of the Bible. While this may be all true, I still had the issue of my anger toward God. I saw the pastor in the hallway afterward and asked him what to do with anger toward God. All he said was, "Don't be." Then he walked away. I was not okay with that answer. In theory maybe things should be that way, but it doesn't deal with reality.

Most people get mad at God at some point in life. We all want to know why bad things happen to us, why bad things happen to good people, and why sometimes good things happen to bad people, like Donald Trump. The truth is we will never know in this life, and honestly, I am not sure it matters. I mean if God did appear to you and explained XYZ about why something bad was happening to you, would that make it any different? Would that make the pain and suffering any less? Would you then say, "Oh okay, God, I get it now. Bring on the pain and suffering. Go ahead and give me cancer. It's cool now since I know why." You still have to go through it.

My father was a chaplain and dealt with pain and suffering all the time. I like his answer better. When I asked him about anger toward God, this is what he said: God can take it. He is big enough, and his grace is more than enough to overlook our rage, frustration, and confusion. There is a reason anger is one of the five stages of grief. I am not the first person to get mad at God, and I will not be the last. I know he will always love me and never abandon me, so it is okay. For all of you reading this who may be angry at God over something, know you aren't alone and it's a very normal thing. I can't tell you how to make it go away, but I can tell you it will be all right.

Great Moment in OCD History 4

I used to have a job as a marketing assistant for an accounting firm. For security reasons, this firm also employed the use of a bathroom key, which has been well established as an icon of obsessive angst. All the employees had their own key, so I was okay with that. I had my key, and absolutely nobody was to ever touch it, lest it be contaminated.

The meeting room was located right by my office, which was close to the restrooms. One day the partners were meeting when one of them came out and asked to borrow my key. "Go get your own," I wanted to tell her, but alas, this was a partner who would probably fire me. Grudgingly, I dug into my pocket and gave her my key. A few minutes later, she returned and handed it to me. I had to touch it.

She then uttered these horrible words: "We need to get you a public key."

"No freaking way you do," I also wanted to say. Instead I managed to squeak, "Okay," even though it wasn't okay. In fact, it was far from okay; it was a virtual bouquet of plagues waiting for me.

The next day the human resources lady came up to me with a key and set it down on my desk. It wasn't long before people started using it, and it was sitting right there, a foot away from me, like a coiled cobra ready to strike at any moment. Eventually I had enough and asked the maintenance guy to put a nail on the wall behind me for people to hang it on. From then on out it hung on the nail, lurking right over my shoulder at eye level like some sinister, diseased gargoyle waiting to pounce on me. Fortunately, I eventually got laid off from that job. I still expect to die from small pox or something.

Chapter 4

In recent years OCD has come to the forefront of public consciousness as more and more is known and understood about it. There have been TV shows about it like *Monk* and *Obsessed*. There have been a couple of movies featuring characters with OCD, like *As Good As it Gets* and *The Aviator*. More people are coming out and stating that they have it. In fact, there are many very famous stars with OCD. Here are a few, along with some of their obsessions.

Howie Mandel—sleeps in a sleeping bag in hotel rooms.

Leonardo DiCaprio—mild OCD, used to avoid stepping on cracks. This is ironic, considering he played Howard Hughes in *The Aviator*.

Cameron Diaz—opens doors with elbows and hand washing.

Woody Allen—obsessed with thoughts of death as it moves closer to him ever so quickly.

Donald Trump—avoids shaking hands, especially with teachers, doesn't touch the ground-floor button of the elevator. Oh, and he is obsessed with Rosie O'Donnell and Mark Cuban.

David Beckham—things have to be in straight lines or in pairs.

Justin Timberlake—straightens things and has to have a certain food item in his house.

Jennifer Love Hewitt—claims she can't sleep unless all cabinets and closet doors are closed while her mother counts the stairs. Of course, she also claims to still have a career and that her boobs are worth five million dollars (this is for real).

The Count from Sesame Street— obvious counting obsession.

Other stars with OCD to some extent include Howard Stern, Alec Baldwin, Harrison Ford, Jessica Alba, Billy Bob Thornton (you knew he had to have something), and Marc Summers (actually he had it bad). Historically there are many people who had or were suspected of having OCD. Here are some:

Nikola Tesla: He had it bad. A big germophobe, he always used eighteen napkins, hated touching round objects, and would do things in threes. He also insisted on calculating the mass of everything he was about to eat, although that could have just been him being a jerk.

Charles Darwin: Darwin had numerous physical ailments and odd behaviors. OCD wasn't diagnosed back then, but most research concludes he had it bad, and was working on a second book, *The Obsession of the Species,* before he died.

Howard Hughes: Everyone knows this one, and it was made even more famous by Martin Scorsese's *The Aviator.* He had all sorts of obsessions. He is also a candidate for the patron saint of OCD.

And while she has never been diagnosed with OCD I am pretty sure Kirstie Allie is obsessed with bonbons.

Other famous names who possibly had OCD include Michelangelo, Ludwig Van Beethoven, Winston Churchill, and possibly both Abraham Lincoln and his wife (Lincoln certainly had depression). While I never heard her name connected with it, I personally think Emily Dickinson had it. She had obsessive thoughts of death (like Woody Allen), and she always left this little tick mark on the papers she wrote on. I once had a literature professor say there was much literary speculation about what this tick was for. I am certain it was because of OCD because I do the same dumb thing. I obsessively leave little marks and doodles on pages. The point is, we OCD types have a history of greatness, so be encouraged.

Despite its public profile, there are still many misconceptions about OCD. Most people don't truly understand how it works. I mentioned earlier how there are two parts to OCD: the obsessions and the compulsions. You have an obsession, and then you have anxiety and fear, so you do the compulsion until it feels right again. We don't *want* to do any of it. We don't want the obsessions or to do the compulsions, hence the term *compulsion*. Unless you get help, you are really a slave to it.

The thing about OCD is that in a way, it's the disorder everyone can relate to, but in a way nobody can. Everyone can because everybody has their quirks, pet peeves, and things that bother them. On the other hand, they don't understand because it really isn't OCD.

I really hate it when I say I have OCD and somebody replies, "I have a little OCD as well. I have to keep things clean." Why do you have to keep things clean? Do you get anxiety because you are afraid of getting scarlet fever if you don't? Obsessions are followed by anxiety that produces compulsions to alleviate it. If you aren't experiencing the anxiety it probably isn't pure

OCD. Liking everything on your desk in a specific place isn't necessarily OCD; it could just be anal retentiveness.

In fact, it can really be insulting to the person who suffers from OCD. I have learned to ignore it when people do this but for many with OCD it can really hurt them. It makes them feel you are minimizing what they are going through. I also hate it when I say I have depression and somebody says, "Oh, I get down really easily at times too." It's like telling a diabetic that you also have to watch your sugar intake. There is validity to your quirks but it's still not the same as having OCD.

Some people think people with OCD are all clean freaks. Ask anyone who has seen my room and they will tell you otherwise. I mean it; sometimes my room looks like a tsunami hit it. It looks like a tsunami followed by a hurricane followed by a gas main explosion. I just like to say I am organizationally challenged. Some people with OCD are clean freaks, but many are not. In fact, for me it is the opposite. I don't want to clean the tub or toilet because they are full of germs, so why would I even *want* to touch them? It is the same reason I never wanted to clean all the soap scum I left around the sink when I was a kid. I didn't want to touch it.

Speaking of being disorganized, there are some who believe compulsive hoarding is related to OCD (although current research may negate that). Trichotillomania or compulsive hair pulling is thought to be related to OCD as well. Fortunately I don't have trichotillomania; I am losing enough hair as is. Although I do sometimes find myself compulsively pulling out my facial hair, I usually catch myself and stop.

OCD offers a diverse and fun range of compulsions for you to choose from and engage in. Here are some of the more common ones.

- excessive hand washing
- long or multiple showers
- checking things (locks, coffee pots, the stove, etc.)
- checking to make sure you didn't hurt a person or animal
- rereading or rewriting
- rereading or rewriting
- repeating routine activities (like going through a door)
- repeating body movements (tapping things, blinking, etc.)
- praying to prevent harm
- saying a certain word or phrase to "undo" something
- arranging things until they feel right
- constantly asking or confessing for reassurance
- sexual or violent thoughts
- repetitive motions or noises

Of course this list isn't comprehensive, and all people adapt their own version of OCD. That's the beauty of OCD; it is the world's first customizable disorder. For instance, under the fear of harming others, you might hit a bump in the road and check to see if you hit a person, or you might have to tap a door in a certain way when walking through it. The funniest obsession I ever heard of was a guy who would check the mail every day because he was afraid of mailing away his daughter.

I have often tried to come up with a good analogy of what exactly OCD is like, and to be honest, it is really hard to describe. Depression is easy to describe. While I can't actually prove this, and hopefully one day I will be able to, I picture depression as something like being mauled by a grizzly bear. One day you are walking along, whistling happily and minding your own business, when out of nowhere this massive beast rises up and brutalizes you. Immediately you fall down under the weight of the carnivore, and you are just left lying there bloody, maimed, and unable to move.

Another description of depression would be like walking along some dark lake, like the one outside of Moria in *Lord of the Rings*. While you aren't looking, some dark, slender tentacle slithers out and grabs your ankle. You try to pull away and fight it, but then another tentacle grabs you and then another as this giant Cthulhu like creature rises up and attacks you. Inch by inch you are pulled into the dark water, and eventually it goes over your head and you drown in it as you are pulled to the bottom of some deep abyss.

One time I was mowing the lawn at my grandparents' house in Atlanta. I was pushing the lawn mower down a slope when suddenly about twenty hornets burst out of the ground, swarming in their stinging fury. Somehow, miraculously I didn't get stung, mainly because I ran screaming like a girl.

To me, that is about what OCD is like. It is like running your mental mower over a nest of mind hornets—and not just regular ones but big, mean, radioactive, communist ones with huge stingers that inject anxiety straight into your brain. They swarm and strafe and dive bomb like a mental Pearl Harbor, and soon you are overwhelmed with it all. You have to attend to each sting separately while all the while trying not to get stung more.

Another analogy is that it is sort of like having a broken record repeating itself over and over in your mind. In fact, I almost always have a song stuck in my head and I convinced it is the same chemical imbalance that causes OCD.

I have always wondered what people thought of people with OCD hundreds of years ago. They must have been miserable and considered insane. I wonder how many old wives tales can be attributed originally to somebody with OCD. I started reading up on them, and here are some of the more fun possibilities.

- Step on a crack, break your mother's back.
- You must get out of bed on the same side you got in on or you will have bad luck

(hence the phrase waking up on the wrong side of the bed).

- To walk under a ladder is bad luck.
- It's bad luck to put shoes on a table (there is the shoe phobia again).
- Knocking on wood for good luck.
- Before slicing a new loaf of bread, make the sign of the cross over it.
- Evil spirits can't hurt you while you are standing in a circle.
- It's bad luck to leave a house through a different door than the one you came in through.
- A fish should always be eaten from the head toward the tail.
- Placing a bed north and south brings misfortune.
- And every guy's favorite—masturbation causes blindness.

Now this last one could just be created by mothers to keep their sons from petting the dolphin, but I could see some dude with OCD thinking God will punish him with blindness for his lust. But if you notice, most of the old wives tales on this list (and many more) involve preventing harm, controlling things, or undoing things, like having to walk through the same door you entered through. That is vintage OCD.

Great Moment in OCD History 5

One day I was helping my dad move stuff out of the storage shed and got a sliver on my finger. Nothing serious, just one of those annoying buggers like a long paper cut that hurts every time you touch something. It was no biggie; I just washed it out, put on a Band-Aid, and later went to work. I was assigned register duty for a while, and you are surely aware by now that OCD people hate loose change. Still, as long as I had my magic Band-Aid on I was fine.

Now I drink *a lot* of coffee, and it isn't a very OCD-friendly habit because it does cause you to go the bathroom a lot. As my coworker said, I have a WB or walnut bladder. In any case, I had to go, so on break I took off my apron and ran to the bathroom.

I entered the bathroom and grabbed the handle to close the door, and that is when I felt it: a dull, throbbing pain in my finger. I looked down at my hand and saw to my horror that my Band-Aid had come off! Time froze, and my stomach churned as panic set in. For all intents and purposes, I had ripped my finger wound wide open and rubbed it all up and down the bathroom door handle, smashing as many germs as I could into it. Not only that, but how many nasty, filthy coins and dollars did I touch? Fortunately, due to numerous computer simulations, I had developed a contingency plan.

First, I washed my hands as thoroughly as I could, making sure to get soap into my open wound. Second, I went to the dish sink and ran dish sanitizer over, also holding it open to make sure plenty got in. It stung a little. Third, I went to the first aid kit and grabbed one of those alcoholic swipes, pulled my wound open, and gently, like a Red Cross worker aiding a wounded soldier in World War I, cleaned my wound again. It stung like crazy.

Was that a little too much? The debate remains to be seen, but I didn't get the Black Death from it—at least not yet.

Chapter 5

OCD really jacked my style for a long time (yes, I just used that phrase). This is not a pity party or anything; it's just an observation on my life. I simply didn't know how to handle it. At the same time, it has shaped me into who I am today. I don't define myself by it, but the way I think and see things has been partly forged by mental disorders. I am told it is often the price you have to pay for being creative. It is like John Lennon said, "Art is only a way of expressing pain." Not that I would go so far as to call this book art.

There are an estimated 2.2 million people in America with OCD and counting and recounting[1] . One of the best things you can do if you have OCD is learn you aren't alone. Go to a support group, sign up for a message board or e-mail list, and most importantly, read this book. It is comforting to know there are plenty of other people, including famous people, out there who are going through the same things you are.

When I was young, I was embarrassed by my OCD. I felt alone and isolated and kept it hidden. Granted, given the nature of junior high and high schools, it was probably a good idea. I was picked on enough as it was, and mental disorders were still largely misunderstood by most people. By the way, where was the anti-bully movement when I needed it? At times I was very, very good at hiding my OCD. When I told some

---

[1] According to www.ocdcenter.org

friends in college about it, they were surprised and said they had no clue I had it. Now I feel differently about it. I am not proud of it, but it is something I am not ashamed of or embarrassed about. It is just a fact I live with. Now I openly joke and talk about it.

The thing is, I have learned a lot about life from OCD (and not just how to open a bathroom door with your foot). I learned that often when I open up about OCD, I find others are more open to sharing their problems too. It builds an instant connection people appreciate. I also learned mental disorders are far more common than you would imagine and everybody has something to deal with. We can't do it alone, though so many of us try.

Everyone has dreams, hopes, and fears. Growing up we all have some idea of how we want our lives to go. I always dreamed I would grow up, go to some awesome Ivy League school, get a posh job I love, and marry a hot wife, all while I collected antique swords (okay, that was pretty ambitious on my part). I learned that our lives never go according to our plans, however. To quote John Lennon again, "Life is what happens to you while you're busy making other plans." Dreams sometimes die, and hope sometimes fades. Nothing really goes the way we want it to.

I learned the universe is not a fair place. I used to get angry at God for allowing me to get OCD. Sometimes I still do. I would cry that it's not fair. Others don't have these problems, so why do I? Then again, it's not fair when people die in tsunamis or that there are starving children in Africa, so do I really have much right to complain? I still get to live in one of the best countries in the world, and I have never been in want for the basic necessities. At least I live in a place where I can get the help I need. It's about perspective.

The problem growing up was that I was an idealist, I thought like a poet. I thought I knew how things would go, and I wanted it all to be fair. I wanted it to all balance out in the end. I wanted to get to be rich or famous or be on TV or something. Developing OCD and depression shattered my illusion of reality. The results were not pretty, but maybe they were necessary. Maybe I needed to be broken. Most everyone gets broken at some point in life. For some it happens early in life while others may make it until they are fifty-five. Being broken sucks, there is no getting around it, but once you are broken, you can be rebuilt into something better, like steel forged in a fire (cheesy analogy I know). It's something that allows you to reach out to others going through similar circumstances.

I learned the healing power of forgiveness and grace. I was very angry in high school about all of this stuff I had to deal with. I mentioned earlier about how I took a lot of my anger out on God, but he wasn't the only one. I also took a lot out on my parents, especially my dad, for the same reason I did with God. I knew they would always love me. That doesn't mean it was right; it was just the way it was.

In retrospect I feel really bad about it. I would get into huge arguments with them, and I would yell and throw tantrums over trivial things. I made life hell for my family at times. At the time I didn't realize what I was doing—that I was taking my anger at the universe out on them.

Several years ago I went to them and apologized. I felt so bad that I broke down and cried in front of them. They forgave me, and that is when I learned the healing power of grace. Because of that, I am closer to my parents than ever before. We now have a great relationship, but it all started with grace. I read once that when a broken bone heals, that part of the bone grows back stronger than before. It is sort of like that. The forgiveness and grace I received from my parents made our relationship grow even stronger in the end.

Most importantly I learned about pain. I learned this world is filled with heartache, pain, and suffering. Nobody escapes it. Everyone gets lonely, and everyone struggles with their own issues. They say love and Klingon are universal languages, but there is another one: pain. I find that OCD has allowed me to reach out to and connect with people on a much deeper level than before. It has helped me get my mind around the reality of pain in our world.

It also taught me that you can't escape your pain, no matter how far you run or how hard you try. I can certainly see why so many people end up addicted to drugs, alcohol, sex, or something seemingly innocent like video games or '80s rock.

Whatever it takes to escape, whatever it takes to kill the pain, if only for a little while, even though in the end it makes it worse. I myself went through a heavy World of Warcraft phase for a couple of years. It was a bad time to be sure. I was lonely and feeling lost, and most of my good friends had moved on in life. I wouldn't go so far as to say I was addicted, but I definitely found an escape in it. It was something to do when I was depressed.

Online gaming can be a dangerous thing. The problem is that you are interacting with others (I was in a guild), and it *feels* like you have friends. It feels social, but it isn't. There is no real community or human contact or touch there. In the end it is a fake community, but so many people get sucked into it. For the record, if you are wondering what I played, I was an undead rogue that loved the battlegrounds (horde FTW). The funny thing is that almost as soon as I reunited with my college buddies in California, I closed my account. I had real friends again.

Let's face it: America is detached from most of reality. We live in this myth that we are supposed to be happy all the time. We live in a world that says money, fame, relationships, success, or any number of things are enough to keep us happy, and they aren't. The rest of the world is very much in touch with the idea of pain. They see it and often suffer from some form of it every day. Whether it is poor farmers in Africa, sweatshop workers in Malaysia, the Dalit in India, orphans in the streets of South America, or sex slaves in Thailand (or hundreds of other places), most people are in a world of pain. In some weird way, our modern society has made our lives worse. We have more stuff and a higher standard of living then a majority of the world and yet we are all miserable. We simply aren't in touch with the idea of going through pain. What is wrong with this picture?

I learned that not only can you not run away from pain, but sometimes you need to run to it. You have to embrace it. You must come to a point where you turn around, look it right in the eye, and accept it for what it is. You can't heal until you do. You can't become stronger until you do. Most of all, I learned that if you turn and embrace your pain, sometimes you find the arms of God there waiting to embrace you back.

The Perfect OCD Bathroom

If I ever got rich—and that won't happen without something crazy happening, and by crazy I mean like one of those e-mails scams about a fugitive prince from Africa who needs my help turns out to be true—then I would design the perfect OCD-friendly bathroom for my castle in New Prussia.

I have written quite a bit about how people with OCD hate bathrooms. They are literally plague-fed pits with more diseases than the Jersey shore both the literal Jersey coastline and the TV show combined. Because of this, I used to dream about creating the perfect OCD bathroom. Here is how it works.

There is one major rule to the OCD-friendly bathroom: touch nothing. To this end, everything needs to be automatic. The door should be an automatic, motion-activated sliding door. The toilet should be automated, as well as the sink, soap dispenser, and paper towel dispenser. Of course, there needs to be a trashcan by the door for the paper towels. Maybe even an incinerator.

Sadly, I have yet to come up with an OCD-friendly way for sitting on a toilet. The best I can do is have a stack of paper seat covers available. I have considered using a bidet, but I am not sure. Besides, what if somebody pranks you and puts ice water in it? To me the idea of squirting stuff up your corn hole just seems wrong.

Automatic is just the beginning. Ideally you would be the only person to ever use this bathroom. Period. To this end, the door would be locked with an optical retinal scan to let you in. Remember, you can't have a key or keypad because that would involve touching it. There would be a good fifteen or twenty feet between the door and the toilet because for whatever reason, I don't like seeing a toilet while I wash my hands. I also never chew gum or eat anything in the bathroom.

Not only should the sink be automatic, but it should also be very large and deep, like a wash sink. The problem with normal sinks is that they are often so shallow that sometimes you bump your hands against the sink. Of course this means you are contaminated and have to wash your hands all over again. You definitely need plenty of space to clean.

There are a couple of other commodities you will want as well. Next to the hand soap you should have an automatic antibacterial gel dispenser for those occasional emergencies. You also need one of those emergency scrub showers, like science laboratories have for when you spill toxins all over yourself or catch yourself on fire. You would run and stand under it while it unleashes a beautiful, cleansing torrent of water/antibacterial solution. The floor should have no tiles so you don't step on cracks or get caught counting them over and over. While not mandatory, surgical masks should be available if the need should arise.

As for cleaning this bad boy, that is where the maid comes in. The maid is the only other person who is allowed to have access to your private panic room. Ideally she would clean it after every use or at least every hour. She would also have to sign a digital log located outside the door to prove she has been doing her job.

Now I know you might be thinking this is a just a little excessive, but I am really just showing you a glimpse of the way the mind of a person with OCD works. It's not like I would actually do this if I had the money, right? Okay, I so totally would; maybe I am better off poor after all.

More Great Moments In OCD History

"Return from Whence You Came!"

Great Moment in OCD History 6

This great moment is a little unique in that it didn't involve my OCD as much as another person's I happened to be around. Here is what happened.

I had come down with a sinus infection and decided I should go see the doctor and get something done about it. While there, I went to the restroom and of course washed my hands thoroughly, As soon as I walked out, this cute nurse called my name and led me back to the exam room. (I would just like to say all doctor/dentist visits go much better if there is a cute nurse involved.) I sat down, and the nurse grabbed my wrist to check my pulse, which had probably just gone slightly up upon seeing her. Immediately upon touching me, she cried out, flinched, and dropped my hand. Now most girls shriek and flinch when they first touch me, so I somewhat expected it, but then she looked at me and asked, "Did you just wash your hands?"

To which I replied, "You have no idea."

We kept up with my examination, and when we got to the part where I listed my medications, I said Anafranil (an oldie but a goody often used to treat OCD). She stopped again, looked at me, and asked, "Does it help?"

"Yes, quite a bit," I replied.

"Hmm, I may have to try it then. I have OCD too," came her response.

It then all made sense as the universe came together in one perfect moment of understanding. Remember, on my list of things people with OCD hate, mysterious, wet substances was one of them. *That's* why she jumped when she touched my wet wrist (at least that is what I told myself). She had OCD, of course! She probably thought I had dipped my hand in a vat of smallpox or something.

At this point I was floored. I couldn't fathom how anyone with OCD could work in the medical field! Needles, blood, urine samples, viruses, puss, coughs, and sneezes are just a few of the biohazards you would have to deal with. To make matters worse, she wasn't even on medication! I thought she was borderline crazy.

I asked her if it was hard for her.

"It's incredibly hard, see?" she said as she held up her hands for me to see how dry and cracked they were from washing too much.

I told her she ought to get on some medication or, even worse, do some exposure therapy. She said maybe, which according to Jack Johnson pretty much always means no. The cute nurse then left the room with me having failed to get her number.

Great Moment in OCD History 7

Unlike most great moments, this one has yet to happen, and as far as I am concerned, it never will. Read on.

I love animals. I love cats and like dogs. Cats are the ultimate writer's pet. You can sit there and write, and if you can keep them from lying on your keyboard, they will just lie in your lap as you type. A cat is like good satire—subtle and thoughtful. Cats are the quiet, comforting presence that is always there with you, even if you don't realize it. Really, they are kind of like God if you think about it. Now the debate rages between which animal is more OCD friendly but in my opinion cats are friendlier than dogs. A cat box is relatively safe to clean. Heck, you can even train a cat to use the toilet (something I will do someday).

I like dogs a lot, though, except small, yippie ones. Growing up we an awesome dog—a cairn terrier named Barney. He was the best, and I have a lot of fond memories of him. For the record, I think the whole not feeding your dog chocolate thing is overrated. One year at Christmas, my brother and I each had three Three Musketeer bars in our stocking, which we placed on the floor and conveniently forgot about while we tore into our presents. Thirty minutes later, we heard a crinkling sound and looked over to see that Barney had eaten all *three* of my bars. And guess what? He was *fine*, but I digress.

As much as I love dogs, I may never have another one. It should go without saying that animal poop is not OCD friendly. When I was young, we made the mistake of having rabbits, and I hated cleaning those cages. In fact, I once told my mom that I wanted a wife who liked to clean cages, so ladies, if you like cleaning cages, hit me up.

Here is why I may never have another dog. Back in the day when you took your dog for a walk and he had to poop, you just found somebody's yard and stood there awkwardly while he did his business and hoped the yard owner didn't notice you. Sure it was annoying, but what else could you do? Oh that's right, you could carry around a plastic bag and pick it up! Nowadays that is the socially polite thing to do. I truly do appreciate it because having random dog poop in your yard is not cool, but I will also *never* do it! I can think of few things more OCD unfriendly than picking up a soft, warm doggie turd and carrying it around until you can throw it away. It doesn't matter if you have a glove or bag, it's still disgusting.

Let's face it—some of that poop is epic! One time my brother made the mistake of owning a golden retriever—not that it was a bad dog, but *his* duty of caring for it largely fell on me. That dog had huge turds, like you need a crane to lift it. I can't imagine having to pick that stuff up and carry it around. A Chihuahua (which I hate) may be conceivable but not a dog that craps like the Rancor monster. So ladies, if you want to marry me and want a dog, just be prepared to do your duty (if you truly love me you will), and if we go walking together with the dog, don't expect me to hold your hand after you touch that filth.

Great Moment in OCD History 8

This is another story about working at the coffee shop. Another one of the non-OCD-friendly tasks involves taking out the trash, which also includes the bathroom trash. Ah, the bathroom again; it almost always comes down to the bathroom. Anything in the bathroom is contaminated, and of course, the trash is filled with used paper towels and other things I would soon find out about. I put on my flimsy pastry gloves and changed the trashes in both the men's and women's bathroom.

On the way back through the middle of the café, disaster struck. I freely admit that the men's bathroom is the dirtier of the two, but I would also submit that the woman's trash is dirtier. So of course if one of the bags is going to burst open in the middle of the café, it will be the woman's trash. I didn't realize it had torn open, and I kept walking, spilling its contents in a long trail behind me. In fact, it wasn't until I saw my co-workers laughing that I realized something was wrong and turned to look.

Horror struck as I realized first, what had happened, and second, that I was going to have to clean it up. I looked at the filthy trail of damp, used, brown bathroom paper towels and shuddered with anxiety. Worse than that, as my eyes followed the brown trail, they were interrupted by something white, square and neatly bundled up among them all. Yep, there in the middle of the café rested that great article of feminine hygiene known as the tampon. By now my co-workers were cracking up at the look on my face.

Don't get me wrong. It was neatly bundled up and all, but this is OCD we are talking about, and I didn't want to even be near it. (If I ever get married, this is one part of my wife's life I want to know nothing about, which probably isn't realistic.) I mean, I didn't want to even breathe the air around it lest I inhale any number of PMS germs, so this was not good.

I went to the back and grabbed the broom and the long-handled trash scoop. I then went back to the trash, took a deep breath, and swept it all up in the scoop. After that I rushed to the back, dumped it all in the large trash can, tied it up, and washed my hands profusely, all to the merriment of my co-workers. Thanks, gang, glad I could provide some entertainment, while I die of some weird PMS related disease.

Great Moment in OCD History 9

I was shopping at a store once and went to check out. Now it must be stated that this chain sometimes hires people that are somewhat—um, how to put this politely—challenged? I won't say what chain it was but if you wanted to shoot an arrow at something their logo would help you out a lot. This is a good practice and I support it, but it can make for interesting shopping experiences. I walk up to the clerk, and he is a very large, greasy, and sweaty guy—the type who has to have a chair to sit in while checking people out because he can't stand for more than ten minutes. In retrospect he might have been sick with a cold as well.

Right when I put my usual bachelor's fare of Hot Pockets, bananas, cereal, and milk on the counter, he sniffed really loud and reached over to a box of tissues. I got a little queasy in the stomach because I knew what was coming next. He held it up to his face and blew really hard into the tissue. Of course after that he had to look at it. He then threw it in a trashcan next to him, looked up at me, and said hi, to which I immediately wanted to say, "Bye!" and go to another cashier, but I didn't. I didn't want him to think I was shunning him for his specialness.

I could only shake my head in disbelief. The guy didn't even use any antibacterial gel or anything! The last thing I wanted was to see was germy, snot-filled hands on my food! I came about this close to calling the manager and complaining, but I figured the poor guy had probably been fired from no fewer than five jobs already.

He scanned the food and placed it in a plastic sack. Fortunately, all of my food was secure in self-contained packages. Heck, that is one reason I love bananas; unlike many other fruits, they have a nice, safe protective layer to keep the germs off. I grabbed the bag and took my food home, feeling rather anxious inside. I had to touch the goods when I emptied the bag, and yes, if you must know, I washed my hands afterward, but still expect to die from malaria, sickle cell or something equally similar.

Great Moment in OCD History 10

Here is another little coffee shop of horrors story and this tale I now relate to you is one of the worst ever. I am not sure how I even survived it. I was closing the store and doing my usual cleaning when the manager turned to me and said those dreaded words that struck fear into the core of my soul.

"Hey, Jeff, could you please clean the bathrooms? And try to hurry since we are behind schedule."

Something deep inside of me vomited bitter bile into the chasm of my soul. Nonetheless, I had cleaned them before, and in theory the more I cleaned them, the easier it would get (this theory has yet to be proven true). So I smiled politely and lied, "Yeah, no problem." I grabbed all the necessary gear, put on the gloves, and proceeded to the pit of doom.

It should be noted that there is no way to clean the bathroom without setting off OCD, but there are ways to minimize it. This usually takes time as I carefully scrub the john while trying not to get too close. However, my boss said to hurry, so I had to try. I sprayed cleaner in the toilet and started scrubbing with the brush, and that is when it happened: the toothbrush effect.

The toothbrush effect is when you have a wet brush like a toothbrush, and it brushes up against something and particles of liquid splatter off. It can create havoc for people with OCD because we fear that particles might fly off the toilet brush, the shower brush, etc.—which is *exactly* what happened to me. But it gets deliciously worse. Out of all the body parts this little splatter of toilet scrubbing juice could land on, what is the worst one? The very one it landed on: my upper lip.

Time froze as an atomic bomb went off inside me. I could feel the heat of anxiety rising up through me. I was paralyzed with fear and didn't know what to do! The fact my boss was trying to get me to hurry only made it worse because I didn't have the time to deal with this properly. It was a nightmare that literally left me on the verge of tears.

When I got done in the bathroom, I threw the gloves off, washed my hands, and splashed water on face. After a good twenty minutes of agonizing anxiety, I finally got the chance to splash dish sanitizer on my face. I then opened up one of the alcohol cleaning wipes and wiped my mouth with it as well. I was even tempted to use bleach if I hadn't been so afraid of poisoning myself. I went home and waited to die of hepatitis A, B, C, D, E, F, and G, but maybe I would get lucky and the cholera would kill me first.

Great Moment in OCD History 11

I mentioned earlier that there was one great moment that was the worst I have ever had, and if you were waiting to read it, your wait is over. It also has a rather humorous ending.

For several complex socioeconomic and geopolitical reasons, the coffee shop I worked at in California had a lot of homeless and transients passing through. Most of them were harmless enough, but we did have a couple of crazies, and one man we had to call the police on and ban him from our store. (Seriously, one day he just ran out into the street screaming and banging on car windows.) Let's call him John. In addition to John, there was another man who we never had any problems with, let's call him Lenny.

It was a Saturday afternoon, I was the shift lead and our store was understaffed, so of course we got a huge rush—I mean like a line to the door. We were frantically making drinks as fast as we could, and the customers were getting impatient. Naturally it was the perfect time for John to show up, followed by Lenny and another guy I had never seen before.

I shot John a nasty look since he was banned from the store, but with the rush we were in I really couldn't stop and confront him then. Not to mention when he walked in, he went straight to the bathroom before I could say anything. When John was done in the bathroom, he walked back outside and waited while Lenny and the new guy each took their turn in the bathroom. When the new guy was done, he walked by me and told me the bathroom needed some attention. I felt a sick jolt in my stomach, but we still had a long line, so I couldn't do much about it. Finally, the line died down and I had to approach my fate.

I was nervous as I slowly approached the bathroom door. I felt like a death row inmate being led to the execution chamber. I stopped in front of the door. It was like a scene from a horror movie. Trembling slightly, my hand reached for the knob. I stopped and lowered my hand in hesitation or more likely, survival instinct. I shook my head and took a deep breath. Lifting my hand, I grabbed the doorknob. As I slowly turned it, the seconds seemed to stretch into hours. As the doorknob clicked, I pulled and swung the door open.

I was instantly hit with an overpowering wave of stench that nearly made me vomit. Suppressing my gag reflexes for the first of what was to be many times, I looked inside. There on the bathroom floor lay the most hideous, foul, disgusting thing I have seen since the *Twilight* series. It was as if a dark portal to the underworld had opened up and hell had spewed its vilest, most blasphemous creation onto the bathroom floor. For you see, there on the bathroom floor of my coffee shop lay a large pile of loose human excrement. Not only was there a pile, but there were smears of it all over the floor and around the toilet. It was like somebody had just decided to disregard the toilet altogether.

This is the part of the narrative where all my powers of writing completely fail me. I can't even begin to describe the anxiety I felt. I felt a cold dagger drive into my heart, followed by an intense heat rushing up through me. I don't know if I have ever had a complete mental breakdown, but if I did, this was it. I was certainly having an anxiety attack.

I slammed the door shut and ran to the back room. I kicked the mop bucket as hard I could in anger. What could I do? How could I possibly clean that mess? And if I couldn't do it, then I sure as heck couldn't make another employee do it. I was literally on the verge of tears.

I wrote a note and taped it to the bathroom door, informing the general public that they were *not* to go in there under any circumstances. It was then that I noticed one of them had tracked some of it out into the lobby.

If I left it there, others customers would step in it. I didn't have a choice. I got the mop bucket and some bleach, put on some pastry gloves, and mopped the floor. I wanted to gag. Then I went back and washed my hands, still trying to figure out what to do about the bathroom. I opened the bathroom door again and nearly puked again. It was *really* bad, like cheap chili had been spilt on the floor.

I ran to the back room, sat down in a chair, and put my head on the desk, trying not to break down and cry. My anxiety was off the epically off the charts. I called my manager, but she didn't answer. I then did the only thing I could think to do: pray.

After a few minutes, I gathered my composure and went back out to the bar. Right about that time, the new shift lead was coming into take over. I told her what had happened, and she, in no kind way, might I add, informed me I was not leaving that mess for her. To which I nearly informed her, in an equally unkind way, that she could piss off. I still didn't know what to do.

I was on the verge of just saying screw it and walking out of there once and for all when salvation struck. One of my co-workers was there talking to her brother. She heard what happened and suggested I could pay her brother to clean it. I asked him if wanted to and he responded, "Yeah, I just got of prison and need some money. I'll do it for twenty bucks." Deliverance came in the form of an ex-con.

I was shocked and couldn't believe it! I ran to the back and got the cleaning supplies. Then I rushed to the register to get twenty bucks before he could change his mind. As soon as he had the cash, I made a dash for the door. I guess once you have been in prison, homeless turds are nothing too serious.

Epilogue

The next day I swung by the store to tell the manager what had happened. She informed me that there is a hazmat service we are supposed to call if something like that happens. I was floored. They did *not* cover that in my shift lead training or I would have surely remembered it. She said it cost around $1,500, so essentially I saved the company $1,480. I then informed her I wanted a raise.

Your Great OCD Moments

So if you have made it this far through the book then chances are that one, you enjoyed it (thanks!) and two, you probably have some Great Moments in OCD History of your own and if you do, I want to read them! I started this great website that you can submit your Great Moments to at:

www.ocdmoments.com

I look forward to sharing in your germ filled anxiety and maybe we can all get a laugh out of it together.

You can also follow me on Twitter:

@nerdy_something

About the Author

Jefferson Jordan was born in Columbus, GA but grew up in Dallas, TX. Now he lives, eats, and breathes in Orange County, CA, though now that he lives there he likes to call it the OCD. He is part writer, humorist, and aspiring super-villain but 100 percent nerd. He writes in a wide range of genres including: satire, comics, fiction, scripts and blogs about life. He loves fantasy, video games, and comic books and every year makes a religious pilgrimage to Comic-Con San Diego. In breaking the nerd stereotype he is also a die-hard football fan. His dream job would be as a late night talk show host. Read his book. It will make him happy and be sure to check out his killer website and blog at:

www.jeffersonjordan.com

Printed in Great Britain
by Amazon.co.uk, Ltd.,
Marston Gate.